AF480653

Who Told You That

CLARENCE BERNARD SKINNER

Published in the United States of America

ISBN 979-8-89395-724-2 (SC)
ISBN 979-8-89395-722-8 (HC)
ISBN 979-8-89395-723-5 (Ebook)

Clarence Bernard Skinner Publisher
222 West 6th Street
Suite 400, San Pedro, CA, 90731
clarenceskinner@yahoo.com

Order Information and Rights Permission:

Quantity sales. Special discounts might be available on quantity purchases by corporations, associations, and others. For details, contact the publisher at the address above.

For Book Rights Adaptation and other Rights Permission.
Call us at toll-free 1-888-945-8513 or send us an email at admin@stellarliterary.com.

In loving memory of my parents, the late Carson and Mattie. Words cannot express the gratitude I have in my heart for all you've done for me. You have taught me the importance of a relationship with God. Thanks for always believing in me even when I doubt myself. I appreciate the insight that words have power to change the world. You are truly m missed. I love you, Mom and Dad!

Contents

Introduction

Communication is a major aspect of survival in this life. If it's done well, we can thrive and become successful. Most of us have not realized how important the way we communicate is. We communicate in various ways. Body posture, tone of voice, and expressions on our face all convey a message. I believe there are five types of communication: verbal, nonverbal, written, listening, and visual.

A word is a single distinct meaningful element of speech or writing, used with others (or sometimes alone) to form a sentence. Our tongue is used to say words. Our words have the ability to build people up or tear them down. They carry extreme power. The words we speak can inspire and encourage others as well as deflate and discourage. They present life and death.

Words being spoken to us, over us, and about us can make or break us. In Genesis, we find that this world was framed by words. The power of life and death is in the power of the tongue, as mentioned in Proverbs 18:21. The words spoken to us and those we speak to others and to ourselves are important. We need to consider our words wisely.

We sometimes choose to allow good or bad words said to us to dictate whether we are happy or sad. This is where most problems begin. We can't afford to let everything we hear and see be the controller of our emotional thermostat. Some of the words we hear can create fear, frustration, and shame. Some words can uplift, encourage, and strengthen.

The book of Proverbs is full of God's wisdom. Proverbs 4:20–22 says, "My son, give attention to my words; incline your ear to my sayings. Do not let them depart from your eyes; for they are life to those who find them, and health to all their flesh." I always encourage others to be mindful of what they allow to enter the heart of their mind through the words spoken to us and the things we see. Essentially, God is telling us to guard our heart from what we hear and see.

1

Me

I grew up in a Christian home where we learned about God, taught about Jesus Christ, and introduced to the Holy Spirit. While growing up, we read the Bible as a family, gathering and kneeling around my parents' bed to pray. We went to church. We were taught Christian values and principles.

My dad was an assistant pastor, and my mother was a missionary and a mother of the church we attended. Growing as a Christian family was significant for us. We attended church often. There was Sunday school and Sunday morning service. We would go home for dinner and rest a little and then return to church for Sunday night services. Throughout the week, we attended Bible study, choir rehearsals, and other events they had planned at our church. It seemed as if our whole life was built around going to church. It was to our advantage because the teaching and experiences advanced our lives.

We had a big family—Dad, Mom, three girls, three boys, and my uncle. Our home had two bedrooms, one bathroom, and a converted garage called the boys' room. It was very small for the amount of people who lived there. We shared the spaces the best we could. Bathroom time was limited. Room at the dinner table was tight, but we always had plenty to eat. Mom was an amazing cook, and Dad was a great provider. Our family depended on God for all our needs. God was our go-to.

Often, in the middle of the night, we would awaken to my parents crying out to God. It scared us because we didn't understand it back then, but we saw the power of God working events out through prayer. I appreciate God for how He allowed my parents to raise us. Everything was not perfect, but we were perfect in Christ.

Growing up, I was considered the middle child among six siblings. They called me the "special one" but not always in a good way. We lived on the south side of town, which we called the *hood*, short for *neighborhood*, where mostly African American— Black—people lived. Our neighborhood consisted of all kinds of people—drug dealers, burglars, and murderers, for example. You could imagine all the experiences we had growing up. Because of how we were raised, we were picked on a lot. Our parents were strict, and there were a lot of activities other kids were allowed to do that we couldn't. This was hard for me.

We were often confronted with situations that go against what we were taught. Everyone had something to say. We never heard of some of this information, and on many levels, this made it difficult when we were growing up. A lot of what was said and taught to us outside our home wasn't how we could live by. If it were cash, it would be counterfeit.

I basically lived on what other people said. I called it "what they said." I believed what other people said like it was the gospel, whether it was the man sitting outside the store next to our home saying, "The sky is falling," or the guy at the barbershop trying to tell others how to deal with their relationships. There were also people at our church who always believed they had a *divine* word for you from God. Let me be the one to tell you everybody ain't got a word.

While growing up, my world was painted by other people's words, from how they saw me, what they thought of me, and who I would turn out to be. I found out early in life that words carry power. The words spoken over me started dictating my life, which at that point I allowed because I didn't know any better. Life was different back then. You basically believed what was said to you. Whether it was right or wrong, you just kind of went with it. Our lives were shaped by the words people spoke to us, over us, and around us.

As kids, we were talked about, picked on, and criticized about how we looked and dressed and the activities we couldn't do that the other kids were doing. I was often told I had a big head, which made me embarrassed when I was around people. I didn't really know how much these wrong words affected me until my more mature years.

Wrong words can put us on a path of self-destruction. I like this quote by Martin Luther: "You cannot keep birds from flying over your head, but you can keep them from building a nest in your hair." Wrong words are the same. They are flying all around us, but we don't have to let them stay and linger in our head. Often, we let the words that have been said about or to us dictate our lives. Someone once told me, "You're never going to be anything." I didn't know it then, but it started to affect my life because I believed it.

I started telling myself, *You're not going to be anything*, and it began to shape my life. The Bible has a lot to say about our words. Proverbs 18:21 says, "The tongue has the power of life and death, and those who love it will eat its fruit."

The right words can get us through a rough season in our lives, whereas wrong words can cause it to seem like an eternity. There were good points told to me as a child that nurtured, guided, and helped me, even to this point in life. I'd also seen how some of the things said to me had caused some areas in me to crash and burn. As a teenager, I was told certain information about how a man should look at sex—get all you can while you are single because if you ever decide to get married, your wife will withhold sex from you. It gave me negative thoughts about marriage, as well as put me on a path to seek out all the sex I could get. I ended up with two children from two different mothers at the same time and at a very young age. I allowed what was said to me to adjust how I viewed marriage and sex.

Many things were said to me about having two kids out of wedlock while only sixteen and a PK (preacher's kid). It caused derailment and dysfunction. Even though I was taught better by my parents, I still allowed what was said to me to take me in the wrong direction.

When I look back on my life, I see a lot of areas where information that was said to me led me in a lot of wrong directions. While growing up, I had some learning challenges. It was hard for me to comprehend. Reading was difficult, and math was hard. I had to repeat the third grade because I just wasn't getting it. My parents had me tested to try and find if there was a dysfunction in my learning abilities, which really made me feel dumb. Through that process, there were many insults and negative comments said to me and about me by other students and the neighborhood kids. It made it very difficult to show up at school, church, and anywhere people knew of me. At some points, I started to believe the gossip that was said to me, which caused me to start making some bad decisions. I would find myself getting into fistfights, making trouble in the classrooms, and talking disrespectfully to the teachers.

These behaviors weren't tolerated by my parents. I would end up being punished at home, taking on more household chores because of my actions. Once, I ended up getting paddled on my rear end by the principal of the school, which ended with a phone call to my dad. And he came to the school. Oh, the terror that consumed me had me trembling. However, I wasn't aware he was coming. When I saw him walk in the classroom door, I almost had to change my underwear. He came in calm and cool like always, asked me to come up to the front of the classroom, and disciplined me by spanking me in front of the class. I couldn't believe it, but it was real. My pride left me, and my bottom was sore.

There were a lot of bad influences in regular school and in Sunday school. You learned to curse, lie, steal, and cheat, just to name a few. It was amazing how people would justify their wrongdoings and somehow make you feel like you could get away with doing them. I was sadly mistaken, causing myself all kinds of troubles by listening to people telling me the wrong actions to take.

I've heard someone say that at least 75 percent of who we are is what's been poured into us by words. Think for a second: there are people who are struggling in life because of abusive words spoken to them—"You'll never amount to anything," "You're ugly," "No one will ever want you," "You're stupid," "You're dumb," for example. These words have caused people to have low self-esteem or become suicidal, angry, and bitter, just to name a few. Resentment and a hater mentality have been part of the list as well. When people tell me negative information about themselves, I always ask them, "Who told you that?" We must be careful about who is speaking into our lives.

2

A Storm of Words

Words form a sentence and are typically shown with a space on either side when written or printed. They often have two meanings. The English language is constantly evolving, and words sometimes acquire new meanings because of technological change. Words also evolve differently in various places. Sometimes they change so much that a new meaning in one place may be unknown or incomprehensible in another. A lot of the meanings of words have changed over time, differing from their common or intended use. Other words sound alike so much that they are often used interchangeably.

Contextomy refers to the excerpting of words from their original linguistic context in a way that distorts the source's intentions. Only part of something that someone has said is used so that the original meaning is changed.

When studying the Word of God, it's important to study Bible passages and stories within their context. Taking verses out of context leads to all kinds of errors and misunderstanding. Understanding context begins with four principles: literal meaning (what it says), historical setting (the events of the story, to whom it is addressed, and how it has been understood at that time), grammar (the immediate sentence and paragraph within which a word or phrase is found), and synthesis (comparing it with other parts of scripture for a fuller meaning). Context is crucial to biblical exegesis, in that it is one of its most important fundamentals. After we account for the literal, historical, and grammatical nature of a passage, we must then focus on the outline and structure of the book, then the chapter, then the paragraph.

Taking phrases and verses out of context always leads to misunderstanding. For instance, taking the phrase "God is love" (1 John 4:7–16) out of its context, we may think that our God always loves everything and everyone with a gushing, romantic love. However, in its literal and grammatical context, *love* here refers to *agape* love, the essence of which is sacrifice for the benefit of another, not a sentimental, romantic love. The historical context is also crucial because John was addressing believers in the first-century church and instructing them not on God's love per se but on how to identify true believers from false professors. True love—the sacrificial, beneficial kind—is the mark of a true believer. Those who do not love do not belong to God. God loved us before we loved Him, and therefore, we should love one another and thereby prove that we are His.

Furthermore, considering the phrase "God is love" in the context of all scripture (synthesis) will keep us from coming to the false and all-too-common conclusion that God is *only* love or that

His love is greater than all His other attributes, which is simply not the case. We know from many other passages that God is also holy and righteous, faithful and trustworthy, graceful and merciful, kind and compassionate, omnipotent, omnipresent, omniscient, and many, many other things. The Bible is the Word of God, literally God breathed (2 Timothy 3:16), and we are commanded to read, study, and understand it using good Bible study methods and always with inspiration of the Holy Spirit to guide us (1 Corinthians 2:14).

Our study is greatly enhanced by maintaining diligence in the use of context because it is quite easy to come to wrong conclusions by taking phrases and verses out of context. It is not difficult to point out places that seemingly contradict other portions of scripture, but if we carefully look at their context and use the entirety of scripture as a reference, we can understand the meaning of a passage. *Context is king.* It often drives the meaning of a phrase. To ignore context is to put ourselves at a tremendous disadvantage.

You've read about the importance of the Bible and its impact, history, and authority. You understand the value of observing the text and learning to interpret what God is saying through it. However, there is one more crucial step to take: putting your knowledge of God's Word into practice.

After washing His disciples' feet, Jesus asked them, "Do you know what I have done to you?" (John 13:12). He wasn't talking about the act itself but the why behind it. "If I then, your Lord and Teacher, have washed your feet, you also ought to wash one another's feet" (John 13:14). Application is where the rubber meets the road, where truth moves from the theoretical to the practical.

A Bible opened for observation and interpretation without application is simply a decoration. As the apostle Paul said, "Knowledge puffs up, but love edifies" (1 Corinthians 8:1). I know plenty of Christians with full heads but empty hearts.

In contrast, consider the reaction of the disciples on the road to Emmaus as they realized Jesus Himself had been opening the scriptures to them: "Did not our heart burn within us while He talked with us on the road?" (Luke 24:32). Their passionate response to the insight they had gained turned immediately to action as they returned to Jerusalem to encourage their fellow believers. Jesus appeared in their midst, "opening their understanding, that they might comprehend the Scriptures" (Luke 24:45) and then sending them to preach in His name "to all nations" (Luke 24:47). To act, though, you must understand both the prerequisites for applying the Bible and the practice of appropriating the Bible for your life.

We are deeply influenced by the world around us. Daily we're bombarded with words and thousands of images—from the news we watch to the sermons we hear to the people we meet. Our affections, attitudes, moods, beliefs, and ultimately our actions are swayed, cemented, and interpreted by the voices we listen to. Yet no voice is as influential in a person's life as their own. No one talks to you more than you do. The words you say to yourself about you, God, and life are profoundly important because they form and shape the way you respond to the things that God has put on your plate. It's true. Whether we realize it or not, we are in constant communication with ourselves—commenting internally on everything we encounter.

We are dictating the narrative we believe with our interpretation of the world around us. And that can be a very dangerous thing.

We all have an internal dialogue whether we're aware of it or not. Some of us may be conscious of it as a constant stream. For others, it might seem less often. Our self-talk matters because it affects our emotions, mood, and ultimately our actions. Put simply, self-talk encompasses both the words we say to ourselves and how we say them. For some of us, our self-talk might include an internal monologue, providing ongoing commentary of our life. Our self-talk could be quite negative, criticizing everything we do. Alternatively, we might speak to ourselves in a positive, encouraging voice, cheering ourselves on. Some of us may speak out loud when talking to ourselves, whereas others keep our self-talk inside our head.

Self-stigma can form part of self-talk. Most of us have heard of stigma—an (often negative) opinion that we develop of certain people or things based on the general views of the society we grew up in. There can be a lot of stigmas surrounding mental illness. Those with mental illness may assume that everyone with a particular diagnosis is dangerous. It's often derived from false assumptions, misinformation, and fear; it can lead to discrimination.

Self-stigma comes from internalizing societal stigma. We hear beliefs shared by those in our society, agree with them, and then apply them to ourselves. For example, we may have grown up in a society that believes those with depression are attention seekers.

With no evidence to dispute that belief, we may agree with it and apply it to ourselves. This can then prevent us from accepting help when we're worried about our mood because we believe that we're an attention seeker who just needs to cheer up. (To clarify: those with depression are not attention seekers, and we all deserve help and support.)

Our self-talk comes from all our experiences and the people we've met throughout our lives. This can include words people have said to us and the way they've said it, films we've seen, books we've read, news we've seen on TV, or information we've read online. The information we hear most often and those that have affected us the most likely stick in our minds most strongly.

"Keep your heart with all vigilance, for from it flow the springs of life" (Proverbs 4:23). This is not a call to speak affirmations in the mirror or boost your self-esteem. It's a call to be careful how you think because thoughts have consequences. As humans, our hearts are naturally deceptive, and our innermost desires are infected with sin (Jeremiah 17:9). Even though God has saved us, we still wrestle with the flesh. That means sometimes we're tempted to preach a false gospel to ourselves and believe the lies we hear. Positive self-talk that discounts reality is not going to help us, but *truthful* self-talk will. That's what it means to "keep our hearts with all vigilance"—we buffer it with the truth. Ground it, root it, and mold it with truth. Soak your thoughts in scripture and surround yourself with honest voices.

Negative self-talk can hinder our ability to learn, limit our growth, stunt our achievement, and drag us down. Positive self-talk tends to empower us, encourage us to try new things, and build our confidence.

As humans, we naturally zone in on the negative. This includes the mistakes we make, things we don't like about the way we look, or *constructive criticism* we've received from others. These can limit our growth and the experiences we have. We may begin to isolate ourselves because we think we can't be sociable. It may affect the jobs we apply for, the things we choose to study, the places we visit, or the hobbies we do. Though we can't necessarily stop automatic thoughts that pop into our head, we can learn to identify how we speak to ourselves and how we respond to our thoughts. The first step is to notice our self-talk. How are we speaking to ourselves? What words are we saying, and what is our tone of voice like? Is it encouraging, or are we constantly criticizing ourselves?

Rather than ruminating over the mistakes we make and the situations we struggle with, starting to think about our strengths can increase our confidence and help us learn and grow. We can begin to see things as possible or achievable, to believe that we are good at what we do, and to look at ourselves as a worthy, valuable person to have around. It can be helpful to find people to speak to about our self-talk. Whether it's friends, family, a professional, or a mentor, other people can often help us reframe our self-talk and find evidence to dispute any unhelpful *facts* that we may tell ourselves. Most of us know someone who has nice things to say about us. Keeping a record of nice messages, compliments, and cards we receive can give us something to look back on at times when we struggle to remember our strengths and to be kind to ourselves.

Positively speaking to ourselves can help us feel hopeful and empowered and believe in ourselves. It can increase our self-confidence and self-esteem. Taking note of our self-talk helps us have an awareness of times when we're being unkind to ourselves. Once we're aware of any negative self-talk, with practice, self-kindness, support, and understanding, we can work to turn it around.

"Finally, brothers, whatever is true, whatever is honorable, whatever is just, whatever is pure, whatever is lovely, whatever is commendable, if there is any excellence, if there is anything worthy of praise, think about these things" (Philippians 4:8). How do we do that, especially in moments of suffering or disbelief when truth seems painful, fuzzy, or far away? We recenter ourselves on the truth of God's Word (Romans 12:2). That's where reality is found. When we're seeking self-talk, we must start with God, not ourselves.

God will keep me. God will bring every one of His children through this life to a better one. He will hold you fast. He will keep you. "For I am sure that neither death nor life, nor angels nor rulers, nor things present nor things to come, nor powers, nor height nor depth, nor anything else in all creation, will be able to separate us from the love of God in Christ Jesus our Lord" (Romans 8:35–39).

God's Word will not fail. That's where you will find truth. Preach this truth to your heart. *That's* gospel self-talk.

Words of communication are so important. Communication reaches people on different levels. It is much more than the words we speak. Communication goes beyond the mouth.

3

How We Talk

A good man brings good things out of the good stored up in his heart, and an evil man brings evil things out of the evil stored up in his heart. For the mouth speaks what the heart is full of.

—Luke 6:45

The way we talk is usually more important than whether we are right or wrong, whether others listen to us, or whether we get our way. In other words, the process usually is more important than the result. This concept is foreign to most of us. We would rather focus on who is right or wrong than examine how we talk. It is as if we were in a court of law, interested only in winning our case. We may be relatively unconcerned about our bitterness, sarcasm, or anger.

How much of our talking is truly edifying or important? Saying what needs to be said is important, but talking too much easily leads to saying what should not be said. Restraining our lips is an indication of wisdom and humility. People who talk a lot often do not take the time to choose their words carefully. Sometimes it doesn't take more than a second thought to decide whether to speak. Many situations, however, are more difficult to navigate. Whether face-toface or online, most of us are constantly subjected to commentaries, conversations, and confrontations. If we're plugged in, it's hard to escape the *noise*. Everyone has an opinion, and most are only too eager to make sure others know what it is. If we're not careful, our reactions and responses can get us into trouble. We all need discernment.

Board meetings, family mealtimes, sporting events, and even a trip to the grocery store can be rife with opportunities to voice our views, ask a troubling question, or offer a word of either encouragement or criticism. At church or on the phone with a friend, we may wonder whether it's appropriate to share a prayer request or a praise report. We may have the right to express ourselves, but that doesn't mean it's always the wisest thing to do. As Ecclesiastes 3:7 tells us, "There is a time to remain silent and a time to speak." When we're not sure which to do, we get the best advice when we search God's Word and receive guidance from the Holy Spirit.

"Please," "Thank You," "I'm Sorry," "Please Forgive Me," "I Forgive You," "I Love You," and "I Appreciate You"

Certain words and phrases make a big difference. Although we know these words are important to say, we often neglect doing so. When we use them, it is like oiling a squeaky hinge.

Talking is often seen as the most common method of communication, but most communication is silent. Gestures, tone of voice, grins, grimaces, shrugs, nods, moving away or closer, and crossing arms and legs tell us far more than words. Learning to take account of these reactions is all part of developing your communication skills to achieve the best outcomes.

Communication can be harder when we can't see these signs, such as when we use the phone, texts, or email. Individuals will have ways of communicating that work best for them.

We are a visual society. Think about it: Televisions are on 24-7. Facebook has memes, videos, images, and so forth. Instagram is an image-only platform. And advertisers use imagery to sell products and ideas. Think about this from a personal perspective: the images we post on social media are meant to convey meaning—to communicate a message. In some cases, that message may be, "Look at me. I'm in Italy," or "I just won an award." Others are carefully curated to tug on our heartstrings, such as injured animals and crying children.

We communicate continually throughout each day. We do it without thinking—we operate on communication autopilot. However, I encourage you to think about how you communicate. How do you communicate verbally? What nonverbal cues do you use when you are disinterested? Excited? Nervous? Are you a good listener? Can you write a concise, clearly articulated message? Are there barriers to how you communicate effectively? Understanding how you communicate is the first step to communicating more effectively.

"A wise old owl lived in an oak; The more he saw, the less he spoke; The less he spoke, the more he heard." Why aren't we all like this bird? It reminds me of one of my dad's sayings: "God gave us two ears and one mouth, so we should listen twice as much as we talk." Or as Jesus's brother put it in James 1:19 (GNT),

"Everyone must be quick to listen, but slow to speak and slow to become angry." Listening can be difficult because it requires humility and the willingness to risk being wronged or misunderstood. Human nature tends toward self-defense and protecting our rights, but a Christlike attitude prompts us to deny ourselves (Mark 8:34). What better example of this do we have than when Jesus stood on trial before His accusers and remained silent except to answer one specific question (Mark 14:53–65)?

Active listening, however, is perhaps one of the most important types of communication because if we cannot listen to the person sitting across from us, we cannot effectively engage with them. Think about a negotiation—part of the process is to assess what the opposition wants and needs. Without listening, it is impossible to assess that, which makes it difficult to achieve a win-win outcome.

Whether it is an email, a memo, a report, a Facebook post, a tweet, or a contract, all forms of written communication have the same goal—to disseminate information in a clear and concise manner—though that objective is often not achieved. In fact, poor writing skills often lead to confusion and embarrassment and even potential legal jeopardy. One important question to remember about written communication, especially in the digital age, is, Will the message live on, perhaps in perpetuity? Thus, there are two things to remember. First, write well. Poorly constructed sentences and careless errors make you look bad. And second, ensure the content of the message is something you want to promote or be associated with for the long haul. What we do while we speak often says more than the actual words. Nonverbal communication includes facial expressions, posture, eye contact, hand movements, and touch.

Effective communication is more than just about exchanging information. It's about understanding the emotion and intention behind the information. In addition to being able to clearly convey a message, you need to listen in a way that gains the full meaning of what's being said and makes the other person feel heard and understood.

Effective communication sounds like it should be instinctive, but all too often, when we try to communicate with others, something goes astray. We say one thing, the other person hears something else, and misunderstandings, frustration, and conflicts ensue. This can cause problems in your home, school, and work relationships.

For many of us, communicating more clearly and effectively requires learning some important skills. Whether you're trying to improve communication with your spouse, kids, boss, or coworkers, learning these skills can deepen your connections to others, build greater trust and respect, and improve teamwork, problem-solving, and your overall social and emotional health.

When you are stressed or emotionally overwhelmed, you're more likely to misread other people, send confusing or off-putting nonverbal signals, and lapse into unhealthy knee-jerk patterns of behavior. To avoid conflicts and misunderstandings, you can learn how to quickly calm down before continuing a conversation.

You can't communicate effectively when you're multitasking. If you're checking your phone, planning what you're going to say next, or daydreaming, you're almost certain to miss nonverbal cues in the conversation. To communicate effectively, you need to avoid distractions and stay focused.

Nonverbal communication should reinforce what is being said, not contradict it. If you say one thing, but your body language says something else, your listener will likely feel that you're being dishonest. For example, you can't say yes while shaking your head no.

When communicating with others, we often focus on what we should say. However, effective communication is less about talking and more about listening. Listening well means not just understanding the words or the information being communicated but also grasping the emotions the speaker is trying to convey.

There's a big difference between engaged listening and simply hearing. When you really listen—when you're engaged with what's being said—you'll hear the subtle intonations in someone's voice that tell you how that person is feeling and the emotions they're trying to communicate. When you're an engaged listener, not only will you better understand the other person but you will also make that person feel heard and understood, which can help build a stronger, deeper connection between you. By communicating in this way, you'll also experience a process that can lower stress and support physical and emotional well-being. If the person you're talking to is calm, for example, listening in an engaged way will help calm you too. Similarly, if the person is agitated, you can help calm them by listening in an attentive way and making the person feel understood.

If your goal is to fully understand and connect with the other person, listening in an engaged way will often come naturally. Give yourself time to think. Ask for a question to be repeated or for clarification of a statement before you respond. Silence isn't necessarily a bad thing. Pausing can make you seem more in control than rushing your response. In many cases, how you say something can be as important as what you say. Speak clearly, maintain an even tone, and make eye contact. Keep your body language relaxed and open. Summarize your response and then stop talking, even if it leaves a silence in the room. You don't have to fill the silence by continuing to talk.

Safely take stock of any strong emotions you're experiencing, regulate your feelings, and behave appropriately. Being assertive means expressing your thoughts, feelings, and needs in an open and honest way while standing up for yourself and respecting others.

Effective communication is always about understanding the other person, not about winning an argument or forcing your opinions on others. Express negative thoughts in a positive way. It's OK to be angry, but you must remain respectful as well. Receive feedback positively. Accept compliments graciously, learn from your mistakes, ask for help when needed. Learn to say no. Know your limits and don't let others take advantage of you. Look for alternatives so everyone feels good about the outcome.

4

Watch What You Say

Most of us have been taught to watch our language and to be mindful of what we say. We learn to be courteous and respectful toward others. This is because words are powerful, and they can have a great impact for either good or evil. Being careful about what we say can affect others' lives as well as our own, not just in the physical world but also in the spiritual realm. The spiritual world is as real as what we see around us.

"Your beliefs become your thoughts. Your thoughts become your words. Your words become your actions. Your actions become your habits. Your habits become your values. Your values become your destiny" (Gandhi).

Words carry the power to move mountains. You can create your destiny by the words you speak. It is very hard to control what you are saying when you are listening, reading, and thinking all day about things that are not healthy for you. We are like a computer; what we put in is what we get out. Our health is much the same way. If all we eat is fast and junk foods, then we will gain weight and sometimes become easily tired. Instead of listening to and entertaining things that are not good for us, we should constantly monitor what we feed on. Philippians 4:8 says, "Whatever things are true, whatever things are noble, whatever things are just, whatever things are pure, whatever things are lovely, whatever things are of good report, if there is any virtue and if there is anything praiseworthy—meditate on these things." If we fill our minds with God's Word, then He will help us in thinking the right things so we can make good decisions.

Words are free. It's how you use them that may cost you. A sharp tongue can cut your own throat. You will not need to watch what you say if you watch what you think. Watch what you say when you're angry. You are what comes out of your mouth. Tomorrow you will have to live with the words you've said.

Before engaging in debates or confronting someone, we should first pray, asking the Holy Spirit to quiet our hearts so we can hear God speaking to us. Then we can turn to God's Word and seek insights and truths that will help us know what to do. Also, the more we absorb and meditate on the powerful words of scripture, the more our own words will be filled with grace and wisdom. We may find that the Lord wants us to remain still, or we may be given both boldness and wisdom to speak up.

Most people tend to treat conversation like a competitive sport, in which the person who says the most, makes the cleverest point, convinces others of an opinion, or even speaks the longest and loudest seems to always win. All of us have this potential. We find ourselves interrupting, speechifying, insisting, and creating witticisms all to support our point of view or display our superior knowledge. If we stop and think about it, though, this approach is the opposite of the one we should take. In most conversations, the person who speaks least benefits most, and the person who speaks most benefits least. The less you say, the smaller the chances you'll share information and later wish you hadn't. It's almost always true that the less you say, the more information the person you're speaking with will share.

Who do you listen to more closely? Someone who never shuts up or someone who speaks occasionally. If you spend more time listening than you do speaking, the people you're speaking to will feel understood and bonded with you. When you do speak, they tend to listen more. My dad used to say to me all the time, "You have two ears and one mouth. You should do twice as much listening than you do talking."

He also said, "You can say more with your mouth closed than with it open."

Throughout the gospels, there was a sense that Jesus never spoke more than He needed to. He always spoke from a place of practical wisdom and was a master practitioner of the economy of words. Jesus understood that words have the power to create or destroy. Most of us talk too much because we have no idea how powerful our words are. If we did, we would think long and hard before we speak. Some may even be compelled to stop speaking altogether.

A good reason to talk less is to truly listen so you can learn from others. Challenge yourself to resist every urge to speak, especially when you're upset or angry. Learn the art of silence.

You may discover some amazing things about yourself and others. Whether you think of yourself as chatty or not, chances are you have experienced the power of saying more with less. "Words are, of course, the most powerful drug used by mankind." Most of us do more telling, advising, convincing, explaining, directing, and divulging than we should. All that talking can cost us time, productivity, and energy. It's also costing us our credibility and some of our relationships. People who talk too much appear to undervalue others' contributions, lack curiosity and selfawareness, and seem self-absorbed and even nervous.

"The most valuable of the talents is that of never using two words when one will do" (Thomas Jefferson).

There are portions of wisdom in the Old Testament that deal with the use and the abuse of the tongue. In fact, the book of Proverbs repeatedly speaks about sins of the tongue and about the blessings arising from proper speech.

"Set a watch, O Lord, before my mouth; keep the door of my lips" (Psalm 141:3).

Other parts of the Bible also give instructions about our use of words. Two of the Ten Commandments refer to the tongue—the prohibition against taking God's name in vain and the sin of bearing false witness. Furthermore, Jesus has warned that idle words will be accounted for in the Day of Judgment. Paul has spoken against corrupt conversation, and James has written about the need to control the tongue. The instruction given in Colossians 4:6 says, "Let your speech be always with grace, seasoned with salt." The word *grace* signifies the idea of beauty and dignity. Although sometimes we need to speak out plainly against sin, we must always remember to speak kindly, charitably, and gracefully—not with a tone of sarcasm. Let your speech be with grace.

In our conversation with others, two kinds of answers are possible, *gentle* or *harsh*. Anger is often dissolved by a calm, peaceful, and gentle response, whereas a severe, harsh, and critical response usually adds fuel to the flame of anger. "A soft answer turneth away wrath, but grievous words stir up anger" (Proverbs 15:1, NIV). The word *soft* does not mean that we should hide our true convictions and avoid standing firmly on moral issues, but we must "speak the truth in love" (Ephesians 4:15). It is hard to argue with someone who insists on answering gently. Proverbs 15:2 says, "The tongue of the wise useth knowledge but the mouth of fools poureth out foolishness." This verse shifts the focus from the tone of our reply (either gentle or harsh) to the quality of our speech.

We can either speak wisely and *dispense knowledge* or speak foolishly and *waste words*. When we engage in conversation, we should talk about matters that relate to living a noble life rather than shallow meanderings that add nothing to the store of wisdom. "A wholesome tongue is a tree of life: but perverseness therein is a breach in the spirit." There are two kinds of words— those that are uplifting and bring life and those that tear down and destroy the spirit. Words, when used appropriately, have the power to heal. Speaking words of encouragement to a downcast person is like a *tree of life*. By way of contrast, words also have the power to crush the feelings of another.

Listening Is an Underrated Skill

God speaks to all of us throughout the day. Most of the time, we don't hear Him because we don't know how to listen or how to tell His voice apart from our own thoughts, the voice of the world, or the enemy. In Proverbs 17, we are given more wise sayings about our speech and about some other very important matters. Verse 4 explains that God is just as much concerned with what we hear (what we listen to) as He is with what we say. We are to guard our ears especially against listening to false and malicious reports about others. "A wicked doer giveth heed to false lips; and a liar giveth ear to a naughty tongue." One of our temptations is to listen to juicy rumors (the KJV uses the term *a naughty tongue*). These are rumors about the failures of others. It is easy to feast on gossip and slander and to believe the worst about others. Countless people have suffered harm because rumors were spread, and those who have passed them along have not bothered to carefully check the facts. We must beware of trying to lift our own self-esteem by diminishing the reputation of others. Verse 4, in essence, says, "An evildoer gives heed to wicked lips and a liar gives heed to a mischievous tongue."

Watch what you say.

5

Everyone Is Talking

So is my word that goes out from my mouth: It will not return to me empty but will accomplish what I desire and achieve the purpose for which I sent it.

—Isaiah 55:11 (NIV)

Words have power. Their meaning crystallizes perceptions that shape our beliefs, drive our behavior, and ultimately create our world. Their power arises from our emotional responses when we read, speak, or hear them. Words are more powerful than we realize. They have the power to discourage or encourage, wound or heal, tear down or build up. Do you ever stop and think about the words you speak and how powerful they are? I challenge you to closely monitor what you say for a day. Notice how many of your words are positive or negative. Notice the effect they have on you and others.

Words carry the power to build. They have the capacity to close the gap between you and others.

You are created in God's image. Like God, you have the power to create with your words. Your words are a creative force. They can create life or death. Your words can build good relationships or tear them down. They determine your future and shape your environment. Every time you speak, you are either building yourself up for the better or limiting yourself for the worse. It's time to think before you speak.

"Words satisfy the soul as food satisfies the stomach. The right words on a person's lips bring satisfaction" (Proverbs 18:20).

"A gentle response defuses anger, but a sharp tongue kindles a temper fire" (Proverbs 15:1).

Many people are compelled to give voice to any passing feelings, thoughts, or impressions they have. They randomly dump the contents of their mind without regard to the significance of what they are saying. When we speak, we should speak with mindfulness to solidify peace and compassion in our characters. Not only do our words matter but the tone that we use also has a huge impact.

There are certain rules that should guide all our communications with others. Always speak the truth. Avoid exaggerations. Be consistent in what you are saying. Don't use double standards in addressing people. Don't use your words to manipulate others. And most importantly, do not use words to insult or belittle anyone.

Speaking the truth and honestly is necessary. We should speak in a loving manner even when we are communicating about our differences and disagreements. We must be lovingly honest. We must discipline ourselves to speak in a way that conveys respect, gentleness, and humility.

Everyone has something to say, but is it viable? Can it create the reality intended? Is what's being said helpful or harmful? Are these words substantial? Can the words be proved through tests and trials?

Our mouths give expression to what we desire, think, and feel. Matthew 12:34–35 says "Out of the heart the mouth speaks. The good man from his inner good treasure flings forth good things, and the evil man out of his inner evil storehouse flings forth evil things." Words are a combination of our thoughts and attitudes.

"People may hear your words, but they feel your attitude" (John Maxwell). Our mouth gives expression to what we want, think, and feel; therefore, it reveals a great deal about the one who is speaking.

It took me almost a lifetime to realize I was giving voice to my feelings, which, in turn, created my reality. If I felt bad about something, I would begin to say it to myself and whoever would listen. I would repeatedly say what I felt. For instance, I was a drummer at my church, and I liked playing the drums. I wasn't the only drummer, and everyone was vying for the opportunity to play, especially if there was going to be a special event such as a choir concert or a special service. I had convinced myself that all the other drummers were better than me. As a result, out of those negative thoughts and feelings, I created a reality of not having the chance to play. I would consistently tell myself that most of the other drummers were better than me.

I was determined to perfect my craft, so I purchased my own set of drums. I was working fulltime, so it afforded me the ability to invest in myself. I was serious about being the best; therefore, I would show up on time to rehearsals and be early to events. I went as far as bringing the drum set I purchased and set them up. But here was the irony: the other drummers would be the ones who played. I would be so excited to play, only to be overlooked by what others considered to be better drummers. They would play for the event, although they didn't attend rehearsals, were never punctual, and never offered to set up or break down my drums. Now ain't that a—oops, I better not say that. LOL.

They were my drums, I set them up and down, I was on time, I made it to all the rehearsals, and most of the time, I had to carry the set back to my car without any help. I felt used, slighted, and rejected. Those feelings consumed me and started controlling the way I thought of myself. I felt as if I wasn't good enough and my talent was worthless. I often spoke out of my feelings, and this was where the problems began.

I began to speak in line with the feelings of not being good enough. My life began to take the form of what I was feeling and saying. I didn't realize then that what I was saying was creating more of that reality. This started to spill over into other areas of my life—my relationships, my job, my social life, and every aspect of my daily interactions. Whenever someone say no to me, I felt rejected. If someone was better than me at something, my thoughts would start going in a negative direction, which affected my feelings and emotions. Then I started voicing those feelings. "No one gives me a chance. I must not be good enough. I don't have what it takes." I realize now words do carry power.

This is how your thoughts create your reality since emotions and the body's reactions are triggered by the thoughts you give attention to. Therefore, you're living in a world of thoughts. Your thoughts create your experiences, and thus, you experience what you think.

It all begins with our thoughts. Our life experiences spring from the thoughts we actively engage in.

When we're unhappy where we are in life, we seek to create change. So we go about transforming our environment, believing that doing so will create the necessary change we hope to see. We buy things for a materialistic boost of happiness. We travel to escape our problems. We seek substances to numb the mind and help us forget. But of course, we fall right back to where we've started, unhappy with where we are today.

And so the cycle repeats itself. We buy, we travel, we forget, always focusing on the external factors we need to alter to create better circumstances. Sometimes we falsely assume that change begins from the outside. In truth, the environment does play a role in changing our circumstances, but it doesn't address the root cause (our thinking) of why we feel the way we do.

If we want to change our outside experiences, we must first change the inside. We must change where we focus our attention because what we think directly influences how we feel. How we feel directly influences how we behave. How we behave defines who we are and what we experience in life. "If you get the inside right, the outside will fall into place" (Eckhart Tolle).

We must begin to understand the link between our thoughts, emotions, and behavior. Thoughts, in and of themselves, have no power. It's only when we actively invest our attention into them that they begin to seem real. When we engage with specific thoughts, we begin to feel the emotions that have been triggered by these thoughts. We enter a new emotional state that then influences how we act. If we regularly engage with thoughts of failure, worthlessness, discouragement, and misery, these will begin to bring us down. Just as with empowering thoughts, they will begin to boost our confidence and thus trigger a more positive emotional state that reflects how our body reacts.

We all have the ability to control how we think and have a better thought life.

6

Check the Source

Before you accept words, advice, and direction from someone, check the facts to verify they are credible, stable, and reliable. I've learned a lot of hard lessons just running with something someone has told me and not checking the credibility of the source. I've seen others judged wrongly, treated unkindly, incriminated, or losing their lives due to incorrect information based on what someone has said. I think this is a major problem with our families, friendships, daily routines, and even church lives. We are often approached with negative and false information that can sometimes cause irreparable damage.

"My dear friends, don't believe everything you hear. Carefully weigh and examine what people tell you. Not everyone who talks about God comes from God. There are a lot of lying preachers loose in the world" (1 John 4:1, MSG).

Scripture tells us not to believe everything we hear but to examine what we've heard. As a young boy growing up, my dad was an assistant pastor, and my mom was one of the church missionaries. We attended church often, more like every time the church doors opened. Church was a very big part of our upbringing. My parents taught us to be very careful whom we listen to and about spreading information we've heard.

Well, church was the last place I would expect to hear negative and destructive things about people. During church, I would hear about people's personal life affairs and stories that probably were not true. It affected how I saw, respected, and received from those people.

In the church I grew up in, people were very judgmental and critical of others. I often told myself, "If they are talking to me about others, I wonder what they are saying about me." There were times I didn't want to attend church because of being judged or criticized. And if you had a past of mistakes, you would be ridiculed and condemned. Even our last name gave them something to talk about.

When I had received Jesus Christ as my Lord and Savior, I became a new born-again believer, and I was really excited about my new conversion in Christ. This was a huge step for me in the right direction in my church. I thought everyone would be happy and proud of me for making this choice. However, a young female member maybe six or seven years older than me came to me at church and said, "You're not saved. You're not a born-again believer." I was in disbelief that she would say something like this to me. It discouraged me, hurt me, and shamed me. It affected me so much I started to believe it. Because of some of the things I had done in my past, she made me feel that God had not forgiven me. I didn't know what I know now, that I am forgiven. What she said bothered me so much I thought I was on my way to hell. For a long time, I carried what she said to me.

Many years later, I began to seek Christ through the Word of God. I read Romans 10:9: "If you declare with your mouth, Jesus is Lord, and believe in your heart that God raised him from the dead, you will be saved." I had met all those requirements, and no matter what anyone else said, I believed I was saved. Listening to that young lady, I allowed myself to be convinced that I wasn't saved. We must check the source and the credibility of the information we're receiving.

How many of us have taken what has been said and run with it, spread it as if it were true, and tainted someone's name or character based on wrong information? I've seen it repeatedly. Someone tells you something about someone they have heard from someone else who has heard it from someone else who says they've never said it. It has gone through so many people's mouths that it's a completely different story by the time it gets out. We need to filter what we hear and do research so we can avoid misunderstandings and the spread of lies. People have had their character ruined by false rumors. Some have made bad decisions about serious issues in their lives based on erroneous information. Life is full of sayings, opinions, and philosophies. All too often, we hear it and run with it as if it were the truth and end up ruining someone's reputation.

How do we determine what we should and should not believe based on what we hear? When Paul has preached, the text says, "These were more noble than those in Thessalonica, in that they received the word with all readiness of mind, and searched the scriptures daily, whether those things were so" (Acts 17:11). The answer, in short, is that one must do research to know if what they hear is the truth. Don't just accept that the Facebook post is true because a friend has posted it, but check it out for yourself to see if it is indeed true. Don't just accept the teachings concerning being a Christian because a friend, your preacher, or even a family member tells you it is true, but search the scriptures daily to determine its veracity. Let's face it: in no realm of life, but especially not in the spiritual realm, should we believe everything we hear.

Jesus encourages us to be *careful* how we listen. Luke 8:18 implies a sense of earnestness, a strong desire, a zeal. This isn't just a casual matter or something optional. How we listen is important, and careful listening is vital to receiving God's blessings.

In your life, remember that God wants you to experience spiritual riches and be blessed with abundance. Ask Him to help you be more careful how you listen. In Mark 4:24, Jesus's words spoken over two thousand years ago are so appropriate in today's world. "Be careful what you are hearing," Jesus has said. "The measure of thought and study you give to the truth you hear will be the measure of virtue and knowledge that comes back to you."

We are warned early in the ministry of Christ to be careful about what we hear. Today it seems people care very little about it. If the preacher has some eloquence and appeal or some sort of zeal, we still need to be careful of what we're hearing. Nonetheless, false doctrine, however appealing it may appear, is always poisonous. Perhaps there has never been a time when people need to listen more carefully to the Word of Jesus in that regard. "Take heed what you hear" (Mark 4:24). Few people will think that hearing anything can be dangerous to their spiritual life. Jesus has also said, "Take heed therefore how you hear" (Luke 8:18).

Blindly believing everything you read or hear can cause you to make poor decisions.

Be Careful How You Hear

Why do some people believe the Bible, and some don't? Why is it that some follow God and bear fruit and others don't?

Mark 4:1 says, "And he began to teach by the seaside." Now this is not the Sermon on the Mount; this is the sermon by the sea. "And he began again to teach by the seaside: and there was gathered unto him a great multitude, so that he entered a ship, and sat in the sea; and the whole multitude was by the sea on the land. And he taught them many things by parables, and said unto them in his doctrine, Behold, there went out a Sower to sow." That means a farmer has gone out to plant his seed.

> And it came to pass, as he sowed, some fell by the wayside, and the fowls of the air came and devoured it up. And some fell on stony ground, where it had not much earth; and immediately it sprang up, because it had no depth of earth: But when the sun was up, it was scorched; and because it had no root, it withered away. And some fell among thorns, and the thorns grew up, and choked it, and it yielded no fruit. And other fell on good ground and did yield fruit that sprang up and increased; and brought forth, some thirty, and some sixty, and some had a hundred.

Now here's the key, verse nine:

And he said unto them, he that hath ears to hear, let him hear and understand. And when he was alone with the twelve disciples and the others who were gathered around. He said unto them, unto you it is given to know the mystery of the kingdom of God.

We must begin to take responsibility for what we hear, how we hear, and how we respond to what we hear. For me, the parable in Mark 4:1–12 creates a myriad of thoughts. Sometimes people can hear something that's negative, possibly not even true, and it can resonate more than truth, giving it power to control, unravel, and destroy their lives. But when it comes to hearing something positive, uplifting, and encouraging, people seem to not hear it. They never get it, or it's just not believable. One of the things I love about God is if we allow Him, He will create in us a clean heart and renew a right spirit within us (Psalm 51:10–19). God comes in and fixes our heart to a point that it is a safe and fertile place to receive the seed of His Word that will increase and yield a hundredfold in return.

Proverbs 4:23 says, "Above all else, guard your heart, for everything you do flows from it." God is telling us here to guard and protect our heart and to watch what we allow to enter in it. The time is now to start setting standards and boundaries when it comes to the *heart of our lives*, the core of who we are, letting the Word of God take priority and fall on the good ground that God has created in our hearts.

God of truth, help us know Your voice amid all the others that scream out for our attention. Give us the strength to hear You correctly and live by Your Word.

7

Other's Opinions

Make it your goal to live a quiet life, minding your own business and working with your hands, just as we instructed you before. Then people who are not believers will respect the way you live.

(1 Thessalonians 4:11–12, NLT)

Mind your own business. Rather than jumping into people's opinions, take time to listen closely to what is being said. If you don't understand, strive to. And if you still don't understand their point of view, ask questions.

We allow other people's opinions to not only hurt us but oftentimes to define us as well. However, it doesn't matter what other people think of us. It doesn't matter what other people say about us behind closed doors or in front of our face. Their opinions have no basis in defining what we're all about.

"Everything we hear is an opinion, not a fact. Everything we see is a perspective, not the truth" (Marcus Aurelius).

People will talk. They always have. And they always will. No matter what you do or say, how you behave, how you walk or dress, how you act, or the decisions you make, you will always be scrutinized by others. It's the nature of people. Like the herd of lions swooping in for the kill, they prey on the weak, looking for those they can taunt and torment, and it gets to us.

Other people have always had an opinion. This is not something new. Early in life, we form cliques. As children, we tend to gang up on others to not only make that person feel bad but also make ourselves feel better. Just because someone is different from you doesn't make them inferior. No one is better than you no matter what, regardless of the color of their skin, their religion, their occupation, or anything else—no one.

Throughout history, people have always found someone to talk about. They've ganged up on those they perceived as different or in some way a threat to their own existence. This is steeped in our society and culture and goes back toward the dawn of modern human. Why do we torment others for no real purpose? Why do we cast out those who are different? What is it about human society that makes this so ingrained into our lives?

The fact of the matter is that people will always convey their opinions and cast out those whom they feel are weak or misfits or simply don't *fit in* with others because they're too fat, too skinny, too dark, too white, too religious, too fanatical, too smart, too dumb, and so forth. At the end of the day, it doesn't matter. People will always find something to talk about. We don't live in a perfect world where everyone is the same, with the same set of skills or upbringings or talents. We live in a wide and diverse world where genetic mutations from the dawn of time have led to a diversity in species on this planet. Within every species, there are countless diversities. The difference is that humans are conscious and aware of their existence and tend to find solace in tormenting and weakening the spirit of others.

No matter what the naysayers and the purveyors of negativity around you may say, your selfworth isn't defined by an approval rating. There's no objective rating scale that allows another person to judge you. They don't know what you've been through. They don't know your story, your trials, your tribulations, or the path you've walked. However, too often, we do allow what others say or think about us to influence how we feel about ourselves.

One reason why you absolutely shouldn't listen to the opinion of other people is that you should trust your intuition. You should trust who you are and why you do what you do. The point is that you must do what's right for you and not base that decision on what other people think about you or what you're doing. Nobody is perfect. Nobody has the right to declare you unfit or unworthy of something just because of a flaw or because you're different from others. If you're doing the right things with the right motives, it doesn't matter what other people's opinions are of you.

It's literally impossible to please everyone. No matter what decision you make, people will always have something to say. Someone is going to have an opinion of which path you decide to take or the direction you're going. They will have an opinion on what you do for your children, what you do for your career, what you do for your education, who your friends are, the places you spend your time in, and what you do for a living. How can you expect to appease and cater to the opinions of people who differ so widely from your views?

However, for one reason or another, we allow other people's opinions of us to dictate how we feel. When we make decisions, and people judge us negatively for it, we question whether we did the right thing. They don't know why you have made that decision. So why is their opinion right? We are all so different. Everything about our lives is different. We're the product of different experiences, upbringings, values, and beliefs. What's good for someone else may not be good for you. Make your decisions for your benefit.

Your path in life is unique and different. Who you are and what you desire is important. Disregard other people's opinions about you. Stay connected to your truth.

People-pleasing turns into squashing your own desires and contorting and molding yourself to fit the idea of what other people think you *should* be. You stop showing your whole personality. You stop feeling like you can be yourself and trusting your own judgment because you assume that other people know better. When other people's opinions are more important than your own, you live life on their terms. However, you're the one who will be left with regret for not having lived a life truly authentic to who you are. They (and their opinions of you) will be long gone, and you'll wonder why you have given them so much power over you.

Seriously, everyone's journey is different, so no one's life will look the same. Often, when we get lost in worrying about what everyone else thinks, it's because we're existing in a state of perpetual comparison. We look at what everyone else is doing and think that unless we're doing similarly, we've failed. We should drop the comparison and just hold ourselves accountable to meeting the goals we set.

Self-esteem is just that—esteem of the self. It's only something that we can give to ourselves. We can only grant ourselves self-esteem. No one else can give it to us. No one else can fill our cup with self-esteem. No one else can say, "Here you go, here's a bag of self-worth." It must come from yourself.

When you overvalue what other people think of you, it's because you're looking for someone else to fill your cup. You're seeking someone else to give you self-esteem. One of the most successful ways to stop caring so much about what other people think is to start feeling great about yourself. That way, you no longer look externally to fill your cup and feel good about yourself. You essentially disconnect yourself from other people's opinions that cause you to feel great or terrible about yourself.

You should set boundaries. If people are tearing you down and making you feel like you're less than they are, tell them, "Unless you can speak respectfully to me, I'm out of the conversation." It seriously can be as easy as that. Set boundaries with those people who have been disrespecting you with their judgments and opinions, and it will instantly help you feel better about yourself.

Remind Yourself Whose Life This Is

Ultimately, this is *your* life. You're the one who will wake up at the end of it and feel that you've lived either a life that is fulfilling or a life that you regret. One of life's biggest regrets is "I wish I had the courage to live a life true to myself, not the life others expected of me." *The only opinion that really matters is your own.* Read that again. Yup, that's right. You're the one who must be happy and satisfied with how you've lived your life. You're the one who is stuck with the results of your life, so you get to decide.

One of the key points about not caring about what other people think is to make the decision to stop caring. It's a simple concept, but it's not easy. By deciding to do so, you're making a commitment to yourself and your happiness and to living your life based on your desires and what will make you happy. That is *powerful*.

A lot of times, we fear what other people think because of what they'll think if we fail. Forget about failure. We don't fail; we learn. What we consider as failures are really opportunities for us to learn. So often, especially in entrepreneurship, we follow everyone else. We do what other people tell us should work because we crave the approval from other people. Or we crave the validation that we're doing it *right*. What's right for them may not be right for you. Your path is unique and different, just like you.

Checking in with the intuitive knowledge about who you are and what you really desire is essential to disregarding others' opinions. Then you will always have a connection with your truth.

8

Thought of Life

Words most definitely affect our thoughts. Words said to us, around us, about us, and ourselves can cause all kinds of thoughts, feelings, and emotions.

Maybe you've heard the expression "You are what you eat." In a natural sense, this statement may be accurate. In the King James Version of the Bible, Proverbs 23:7 seems to suggest a different but related truth—that we are what we think: "For as he thinketh in his heart, so is he." Although this scripture has a deeper meaning to it considering its context, let's use it. So, what are you thinking?

A positive thinker is taking an optimistic approach toward life. They are, in general, people who look on the bright side and will take responsibility for their own lives, actions, and feelings rather than blame others or external events. A positive thinker will not be deterred by challenging events in their life. Instead, they will consider what is learned from them and how to best apply this learning going forward.

Positive thinking does not mean that a positive thinker will never be sad or angry. However, they are likely to channel these feelings in healthy ways and may use them as motivators for change. A positive thinker will generally display a greater sense of self-worth and do their best to achieve what they want in life.

Another aspect of positive thinking is accepting that there is always room for improvement and taking steps to achieve this. Positive thinking alone does not guarantee success. Without completely understanding what it means and how it works, it can give us a false sense of reality.

One study has found that a habit of prolonged negative thinking diminishes your brain's ability to think, reason, and form memories, essentially draining your brain's resources. Another study has reported in the *American Academy of Neurology Journal* that cynical thinking also produces a greater dementia risk.

Everyone knows that negativity is psychologically bad. For instance, negativity has been associated with poor memory, a decrease in perception, and even limited reasoning and logic skills. Furthermore, severe negativity has been known to cause depression and even suicide. Additionally, negativity has also been proved to be physically harmful. For instance, negativity can cause loss of appetite and thus lead to skin and internal organs becoming anemic. In some extreme cases, negativity is believed to have even led to death. Therefore, I think everyone can agree that negativity has been proved to be harmful.

Did you know your thoughts dictate your feelings? Feelings and emotions are a result of chemical reactions taking place in your body. These reactions are responsible for negative emotions such as anger and sadness, as well as positive feelings such as love and happiness. So, it makes sense that to overcome negative thoughts, you must change your thought pattern, otherwise known as *thought stopping*.

Therefore, the only solution is to always be aware of the amount of negativity inside each of us and their effects around us. Then we will be able to make minor adjustments to our mental health whenever necessary. These adjustments may mean a short break, a long relaxing lunch, or even a much-needed vacation far away from everything stressful.

So you may want to ask yourself these questions: Are you too negative? Or are you too positive? If you answer yes to either question, what are you going to do about it?

Philippians 4:8 says, "Finally, brethren, whatever things are true, whatever things are noble, whatever things are just, whatever things are pure, whatever things are lovely, whatever things are of good report, if there is any virtue and if there is anything praiseworthy—meditate on these things."

The Bible tells you plainly that God wants you to "prosper in all things and be in health." And *all things* covers *all*, meaning that even when you think something is small and seemingly insignificant, it is significant to God. He wants you to experience success even in that area!

You may be thinking, *Does God really bother about what's going on in my life when He's got an entire universe to run?* It may surprise you, but He does. He even keeps track of the number of hairs on your head (see Luke 12:7). So just imagine how much more God cares about the matters important to you, however big or small they are. If it's troubling you, He wants to take care of it.

The Word of God is living and active. If you confess the Word of God over your heart and life, it will not return void.

The thoughts and inclinations of the heart shape the reality of who you are. They shape your thinking, which will ultimately shape your actions. That's why what you think matters because it is forming the basis of who you will become. If you need to know who a person really is, you can't always determine that by the words they say. You must look at the root of who they are, and that is the heart. Everything a person is flows out of their heart.

Jesus says you will know a tree by its fruit. The fruit of the tree is simply a reflection of the root it's connected to. You will never get an orange from an apple tree root. The core of who you are is evidenced by the thoughts or roots of your heart. That's why what's on the inside is so much more important than what's on the outside. You can mask the outside from others, and you can try to bury it, but ultimately, what's in your heart will reveal who you really are.

Constantly, a lot of information is being thrown at us in the form of words, constructive and positive, some given in error. Social media, television, and the newspaper are just a few ways we receive information that can significantly shape how we think.

As a kid, I watched and listened to some of the great musicians around me and the ones who had recordings. Thoughts of becoming a musician became a focal point. The thought got so big I started inquiring about learning how to play music on several different instruments. That led to spending countless hours practicing and performing. All this led me to becoming a music producer. My thoughts were shaped by what I saw and heard.

Let's look at the idea of taking advice about marriage from a person who has never been married. The dilemma is what we are taking in and what we are allowing ourselves to ponder on. Our minds will dictate our actions. The good words spoken to us can encourage us, build us up, give insight on solutions to problems, and possibly persuade a suicidal person to live and not die. The bad words said to us can discourage us, lead us in the wrong direction, and stunt our growth in life.

God has given us a mind to think. It's our responsibility to control what we think. One of my favorite scriptures is 2 Corinthians 10:5: "Casting down imaginations, and every high thing that exalteth itself against the knowledge of God and bringing into captivity every thought to the obedience of Christ." What we allow to capture our mind and heart is what will determine our outcome in the situations of life.

Words and thoughts are so important because they form images. Often, the words you hear strengthen the thoughts or images that you entertain. If negative and doubt-filled words are what you hear, then it strengthens those thoughts. If positive and faith-filled words are what you hear, then it strengthens those thoughts. The images that you receive cause you to believe, and thus manifest through your faith, the imaginations that you entertain with your thought life.

You must cast down and not exalt images that try to be above the Word of God. Whatever imagination or image you receive and believe becomes empowered by your faith, and will soon manifest, if you keep exalting it. Again, you must begin to declare

God's images (vision for you and about you and your circumstances), even in the face of a circumstance that may look totally opposite of what you are saying. What the Word of God says is God's image (vision) for you. Begin to declare it and immediately cast down from your mind any thoughts that are contrary to what God has said.

The Word of God is not just a beautiful piece of literature to be savored and enjoyed. Its purpose goes beyond provoking thought and inviting meditation. It requires more than memorization and sharing with others. It demands a change of heart that prompts a change of behavior.

There's a lot to say about our thought life. Words play a major part in how we think. Words said to us and what we say to ourselves get deposited inside us.

9

Self-Pity

Self-pity is excessive, self-absorbed unhappiness over one's own troubles. It is a slimy, bottomless pit. Once you fall in, you tend to go deeper and deeper into the mire. As you slide down that slippery slope, you are well on your way to depression, and the darkness is profound. Your only hope is to look up and see the light of God's presence shining down on you. Though the light looks dim from your perspective deep in the pit, those rays of hope can reach you at any depth. While you focus on and trust God, you will slowly rise from the abyss of despair.

We all know people who wallow in self-pity. In fact, each of us has had times when we feel sorry for ourselves. We figure that of everyone we know, we are the most miserable, our circumstances are bad, everyone hates us, and we can never do anything right. Those thoughts and feelings make us miserable.

Such thinking is selfish and wrong. What makes us think we are the only ones who have ever suffered? Deep down, we know that everyone is not against us. Even if it were true, God is for us.

Self-pity shows a lack of trust in God. Before you start feeling sorry for yourself, remember that the condition is common. There was a time when the great prophet Elijah told God that he was so bad off that he would rather die than live (1 Kings 19). God responded by reminding Elijah that God was still with him and that things were not as bad as Elijah made them seem.

Sadly, for some people, pity is the only *positive* affirmation they think they can receive from loved ones. This can make it challenging for them to want to overcome it. It can act as a mental anesthesia that numbs the pain in a way, yet the person stuck in it is unwilling to properly address or deal with whatever is causing the pain.

Every human being is prone to self-pity. We are born self-centered with a powerful drive to protect our ego and our rights. When we decide that life has not treated us as we have the right to be treated, self-pity is the result. It causes us to sulk and obsess over our hurts, real or perceived. At the heart of self-pity is a disagreement with God over our life and how we feel He has treated us.

Self-pity tends to emphasize egocentric feelings of separation from others and exaggerate the extent of personal suffering. Self-compassion, on the other hand, allows one to see the related experiences of self and others without the feelings of isolation and disconnection. Also, selfpitying people often become engrossed in their own emotional drama. They cannot step back from their situation and adopt a more balanced or objective perspective.

A strange situation you suddenly find yourself in may be one of the most difficult challenges you've faced in life. The way you choose to respond to it may have a huge impact on your future. You have two choices: figure out how to make the best of the situation or let yourself sink into self-pity. Clearly, choosing to feel sorry for yourself can have some serious consequences.

Self-pity will keep you stuck in an unhealthy cycle of negative thoughts, uncomfortable feelings, and inactivity. It will drain you of the mental strength you need to approach this challenge at your best. Self-pity can cause you to imagine worst-case scenarios—such as your life being ruined. That way of thinking becomes self-destructive because you will likely grow to believe there isn't anyone or anything that can help you feel better. When you reach this point, you start to believe that any effort you put into changing your life is useless, so you won't take any action at all. You will stay in your dark place, and the cycle repeats as you spiral further downward. The worst you feel, the more negative your thoughts will be. The more negative thoughts you have, the less likely you are to take action. Inactivity leads to more dark feelings.

How can you prevent falling into self-pity? How can you stop feeling sorry for yourself so you can take necessary action?

Act Contrary to How You Feel

If you feel yourself heading down the road of self-pity, it's easy to let yourself continue in that direction. Rather than work on figuring out solutions to your problems, you will waste time by taking the easy way out and assuming that nothing will work. If you find yourself focused on the unfairness of circumstances, you will probably start complaining to family, friends, and whomever you meet. Your complaints might gain momentary sympathy from some, but right now, everyone has problems of their own.

Think about it. Has anyone ever said to you, "What I really like about you is that you always complain about your problems and feel sorry for yourself"? Of course not. And you likely don't enjoy the company of others with this attitude either. Commiserating isn't exactly a very good bonding activity. We should remain positive and build one another up now more than ever.

It's important to alter your behavior and actions. Do things that make it more difficult to wallow in your unhealthy thoughts and emotions. This may involve getting up off the couch and get moving. Physical activity is so important for your emotional and mental health. It will probably be more difficult during this time, so you may have to be creative. Depending on the restrictions where you live, you may be able to go out to walk. You may also do something kind for others. Help a friend or volunteer for a charity. There are plenty of people in need right now whom you can help. Kind acts remind you how much you can give to others.

Exchange Self-Pity for Gratitude

Self-pity causes you to think, so the easiest way to conquer feelings of self-pity is to change the way you think. A feeling of gratitude offers a variety of benefits, including better sleep, improved health, better stress resilience, and more mental strength. Every time you are tempted to complain about how bad your situation is, think about three things you're grateful for. Some people even take it a step further and write them down. When you begin to realize how much you have to be thankful for, you'll be much less likely to slide into self-pity.

Rejecting the impulse to feel sorry for ourselves is not easy. Life provides many opportunities to experience rejection, injustice, and the cruelty of humans. Our natural response is self-protection, which often results in self-pity.

A cure for self-pity is to quit looking inward. It's not all about you or me. Self-pity is, at its heart, self-centered. Also quit looking around at others. Someone else always has it better, and someone else always has it worse. Rather than looking inward or outward, we ought to be looking upward. This is the one and only way to rid ourselves of self-pity and be truly happy.

"Trust in the Lord and do good; dwell in the land and enjoy safe pasture. Delight yourself in the Lord and he will give you the desires of your heart" (Psalm 37:3–4).

To be overcomers, we need to be willing to submit every thought, pattern of behavior, and selfwill to God, holding it up to the light and recognizing its source. We also need to be willing to cast all our cares on God so that He can begin to start bringing true healing to our hearts. "Casting all your care upon Him, for He careth for you" (1 Peter 5:7, KJV).

10

Trusting

Many of us were taught from our early experience that we need to protect ourselves from others. While serious issues of abuse and neglect are clearly deeply harmful, even the bestintentioned parents hurt their children. They reply sharply, they don't notice the distress of their kids, they tell their kids how they should feel, and they sometimes misunderstand what their kids' needs are. Parents are human too; they are preoccupied, and they have their own hang-ups and patterns.

Unfortunately, when we're young, we don't have this perspective. Many of us quickly internalize that we need to look out for ourselves, protect ourselves, and not trust others. After all, they might just let us down. This usually gets ingrained so early that we don't know there's another way. We believe this is just *how the world works*.

This belief stays with us into adulthood and often gathers more evidence. We get more sophisticated about it—we learn how to have relationships with others, whom we keep at arm's length, ensuring we can still protect ourselves. Our core relational template is that others cannot be trusted, and we need to look out for ourselves. While understandable, this belief doesn't lead to deep, healthy, vulnerable relationships, which are what Jesus calls us to have as one of the primary ways He weaves His joy, fulfillment, purpose, and peace into our lives.

As we travel through this broken, beautiful world, we will be hurt. It's a simple fact of living in the land of imperfect people and systems. We often have many reasons not to trust based on our own experiences and relationships. If we don't work through our hurt with Jesus, we let each one become a barricade to our hearts. Each experience with a flawed person becomes another reason not to trust. Unfortunately, all those barricades leave you alone, and it is not good for man to be alone (Genesis 2:18).

We are called to forgive from the heart, clearing those barricades we've set up to guard ourselves. This may sound impossible and, depending on the very real pain we've experienced, unfair and unfeeling. But Jesus is the expert at this. He's walked this road to get to us, and He can lead us along it too. You have not been made to have a hardened, barricaded heart. You have been made to have a soft, compassionate, trusting heart that is filled and protected by the Holy Spirit.

Most of us are walking around with unspoken, unclear, and potentially unrealistic expectations of those around us. We may not be aware of our expectations until someone fails us. This is a recipe for hurt and broken relationships. One way this comes out is when we expect others to love or care for us in the same way we care for them. We get hurt when our friends or family don't express their love for us in the same way we express it, and we internalize that as we can't trust them.

Sometimes it's awkward and difficult to have conversations about our expectations. It takes courage and self-awareness because if we aren't aware of our expectations, it's hard to convey them to someone else. But if we carry around unspoken expectations, it's only a matter of time before our trust feels flimsy, unbeknownst to the person on the other side. So choose to step out in courage and communicate your expectations.

On the Other Hand

When you think about it, we sure do trust a lot of man-made things that can fail us at any moment, for example, our cars and other high-tech transporters such as trains and airplanes. Think about the latter for a second. We willingly put ourselves in a metal can that hurtles through the sky at 500+ mph, at a commercial cruising altitude of 35,000 feet. That's a long fall to the ground if the wing snaps or the engine fails.

We put our trust in traffic lights, stop signs, and the blinking walk sign at crosswalks. We trust that the bank will return our money to us when we want it. The bank itself trusts us to pay off our credit cards and house loans. That trust isn't always rewarded.

Also, we trust our well-being, if not our very lives, to other people. Every time we step into a new relationship, we open ourselves up to potential joy and chest-crushing pain. Even when we open our arms to offer a hug, we expose our heart to rejection.

Some of us trust in philosophies so bizarre that they require not only our blind faith but also our total dismissal of reality. Critics like to say that Christians do both, but their claims lack truth. Christianity isn't bogus; it's based on vetted historical facts and the very real personage of Jesus.

Lastly, most of us put a ton of trust in ourselves. We've been influenced by society to believe that our individual fates are entirely due to our own efforts.

Primarily through our increasingly secular media and educational systems, we've been conditioned away from trusting God and toward trusting in the inherent power of humanity. We have no idea just how immoral we've become. As I've overheard one person say, "We don't even know what immorality is anymore."

11

Confidence

So do not throw away this confident trust in the Lord. Remember the great reward it brings you! Patient endurance is what you need now, so that you will continue to do God's will. Then you will receive all that he has promised.

—Hebrews 20:35–36 (NLT)

For I can do everything through Christ, who gives me strength.

—Philippians 4:13 (NLT)

I don't think I know a single person who doesn't want to come across as confident. But appearing confident and being confident are two different things. True confidence comes from within. We feel it in ourselves. It is communicated through gestures, in how we carry ourselves, and in what we say to others.

A person who isn't truly confident often wants to be seen as such. They're afraid others don't take them seriously, so they try to overcompensate. Confident people, on the other hand, aren't afraid to answer questions honestly including when they don't know.

There's a perception that to be a good leader, you need to know the right thing to do all the time. This is fallacy. You don't need to already know; you need to be willing to discover what it is. You need to be able to listen closely to those who are more educated on the subject than you and then call the shot.

Confidence isn't about having all the answers; it's about being comfortable and seeking them out. Insecure people are often unwilling to say "I'm sorry" because they perceive it as weakness. They do everything they can to blame others instead of taking any responsibility themselves. They're terrified that if they say something like "I was wrong," what they're saying is, "I'm bad." Confident people, on the other hand, are able to say, "I'm sorry. I didn't realize that what I said had that impact. I'd like the opportunity to do better next time." Apologizing when you've made a mistake is the trait of a confident person.

No is a complete sentence. It's also one of the hardest sentences to learn how to say, particularly if you have been raised in a home where saying no is not allowed. If it hasn't been safe for you to assert healthy boundaries as a child (or if you have been punished for doing so), you often become a people pleaser as an adult.

Let's face it: most people have poor boundaries. It takes practice to learn how to say yes only when you mean it and how to say no tactfully but firmly. Confident people practice good boundaries. They say no when they need to. They trust that others won't attack them for saying no and understand that if someone does push back on their boundaries in a disrespectful way, that person is in the wrong, not them.

Research conducted at the University of California in San Francisco shows that the more difficulty you have saying no, the more likely you are to experience stress, burnout, and even depression. Confident people know that saying no is healthy, and they have the self-esteem to make their noes clear.

Confidence stems from connections. When you know you're truly connected to others and when there are people with whom you feel safe to be fully yourself, you're able to take risks. You're willing to put yourself out there because you know if you fall on your face, someone will have your back. Confidence can help you achieve a successful life.

Henry Ford said it best. "Whether you think you can or think you can't, you are right." Ford's notion is that your mentality has a powerful effect on your ability to succeed.

Happiness is a critical element of confidence because to be confident, you must be happy with who you are. People who brim with confidence derive their sense of pleasure and satisfaction from their accomplishments, as opposed to what other people think of their achievements. They know that no matter what anyone says, they're never as good or bad as people say they are. Comparing oneself to other people is limiting. Confident people don't waste time sizing people up and worrying about whether they measure up to everyone else.

People with confidence listen more than they speak because they don't feel like they have anything to prove. Confident people know that by actively listening and paying attention to others, they are much more likely to learn and grow. Instead of seeing interactions as opportunities to prove themselves to others, they focus on the interaction itself because they know this is a far more enjoyable and productive approach to people.

It's difficult to get people to listen to you if you can't deliver your ideas with conviction. People are sometimes turned off by those who are desperate for attention. Confident people know that being yourself is much more effective than trying to prove you're important. They don't crave the approval or praise because they draw their self-worth from within.

Confident people aren't afraid to be proved wrong because they learn a lot from the times they are wrong, and other people learn from them when they're right. They know that asking others for help won't make them seem weak or unintelligent. They know their strengths and weaknesses, and they look to others to fill the gaps. They also know that learning from others with more expertise is a great way to improve.

Building trust in yourself can help boost your decision-making skills and self-confidence. Building confidence is a journey, not a destination.

12

If God Said It ...

God is not a man, that He should lie, nor a son of man, that He should repent. Has He said, and will He not do it? Or has He spoken, and will He not make it good *and* fulfill it?

—Numbers 23:19 (AMP)

The One who called you is completely dependable. If He said it, He'll do It.

—1 Thessalonians 5:24 (MSG)

God's word can be trusted. He has a lot to say about life that encourages better living. I've found Him to be a waymaker when there seems to be no way. God's word is life. So often, we look for words of affirmation and encouragement, words to lead, guide, and make us feel good about ourselves. Sometimes it's possible to overlook the One who has created us, the One who knows all about us and has spoken into our lives.

Where We Sometimes Go Astray

People say all the time that life is flux. There are constant changes: life, relationships, jobs, residences—the list can go on and on. Friends drift in and out of our lives, ambitions are frustrated, and dreams die. In the middle of life, hair turns gray, skin starts to sag, waistline expands, loved ones die, and decades pass like years. We see all these in life, and without God's insight, they can look gloomy.

A lot of intelligent and thoughtful people struggle with the questions about a God who is allgood, all-powerful, and all-knowing. They feel and wonder how a God like this can fail to meet their expectations or do what they want. People often wonder why bad events happen. Why does God allow suffering? They ask the question Does God even care? Why doesn't God do anything about it? God cares, sees, and knows everything. He even knows the number of hairs on your head (Luke 12:7).

Everyone experiences disappointment or sadness to some degree. In Psalm 13, David demonstrated what it means to trust in tough times. Feeling forgotten, forsaken, sorrowful, and subdued, David cried out for God's consideration and illumination. As he prayed, his perspective changed, and he was able to rejoice, although his circumstances remained the same. When we face difficult times, we must resist self-pity, trusting that God knows what's best for us, and He can use our hard experiences for good.

Often, we may find ourselves asking God questions like David did. "How long will You forget me? How long will You forsake me? How long will You hide Your face from me?" David felt left out, misplaced, and forgotten. If we're honest, this is a feeling with which each of us can identify. It may not be what we are thinking right now but maybe a week or two or a year ago. If we have not had reason to feel this way, if we just live a little longer, we will have the opportunity.

In this season of life, we must remain diligent in trusting God and believing what He has said in His promises to us. He has said, "I will not leave you or forsake you" (Hebrews 13:5). All of God's promises are received through believing them. Believing means to receive, and to receive means to believe. The Bible teaches us that we receive what we believe.

We need to believe and keep this in the forefront of our mind, even when everything seems to change, people walk away, and life seems to be completely out of control. God is our everpresent help in times of trouble (Psalm 46:1).

We Need to Learn to Agree with God and to Say What He Says

Have you ever had anyone making a promise to you and then breaking it before the words ever crossed their lips? Have you ever been told, "I'll be there for you," or "I have your back," only to find the so-called promise maker not delivering?

We all must realize people are humans with flaws and will let you down. Never in the history of the world have words been cheap, quick, irrevocable, and viral. People's reputations have been destroyed by what others have said, and yet their words hold no truth at all. We are having a word explosion, and we have yet to see what damage will be caused by it unless people learn the power of words and make a commitment to use them with discretion and respect.

Our words are not forced on us. They formulate in our mind, and then we speak. Words are wonderful when used properly. When we understand the power of words and choose what we think and speak, our lives can be transformed.

"A good man eats good from the fruit of his mouth" (Proverbs 13:2). As we see, we eat our words, and we can rightfully say that they are food for our souls.

Can we control what comes out of our mouths? It's almost impossible to tame our tongue without God's help.

"People can tame all kinds of animals, birds, reptiles, and fish, but no one can tame the tongue. It is restless and evil, full of deadly poison. Sometimes it praises our Lord and Father, and sometimes it curses those who have been made in the image of God. And so, blessing and cursing come pouring out of the same mouth. Surely, my brothers and sisters, this is not right!" (James 3:7–10, NLT).

We Must Learn to Say What God Says

We cannot say what God says unless we know God and what He has said. Therefore, we must study and listen to the words of God diligently. We must get to know God to understand what to expect from Him. We must know His Word because God and His Word are one. It is not possible for God to say one thing and do another. He cannot lie and is always faithful to perform what He has promised.

13

Put It on Repeat until You Get It

How then will they call on Him in whom they have not believed? And how are they to believe in Him of whom they have never heard? And how are they to hear without someone preaching?
And how are they to preach unless they are sent? As it is written, "How beautiful are the feet of those who preach the good news!" But they have not all obeyed the gospel. For Isaiah says, "Lord, who has believed what he has heard from us?" So faith comes from hearing, and hearing through the word of Christ.

—Romans 10:14–17

Have you ever rewatched a movie and seen things you have missed the first time? I have often read or listened to materials repeatedly to make sure I have received and understood it correctly. I have listened to teachings multiple times to ensure I have received all the information.

As we read Romans 10:17, we see that Paul is saying that faith comes to a person when the good news of the Gospel is preached to them and then believe this good news they have heard: "Faith comes from hearing, and hearing through the word of Christ."

When I think of hearing, my first impression is it comes by an auditory method. However, hearing means more than using our ears. Hearing implies speaking, yet the impartation of a message by any means of direct communication (e.g., reading) can be considered speaking (1 John 5:13). So can a deaf person come to faith? By all means. They do not hear with their ears, but they hear with their intellect and with their hearts as they either interpret sign language or read the Bible. They make decisions based on the truth of what they hear. Has anyone currently heard Moses, Matthew, or Jesus with their ears? No, yet when we read, it is as if they are speaking to us.

The writers in the Bible were moved by the Holy Spirit (2 Timothy 3:16–17). They spoke in past ages, yet we still hear their voices through their writings today (Hebrews 1:1 and John 17:20).

Hearing Is Key to Faith

One word from God can change your whole life. It can change your situation. It's important that as Christians we know it's not just about wearing a Christian T-shirt but also about having a personal, ongoing, everyday relationship with God. Part of that relationship is not just you talking to Him but also giving Him an opportunity to talk to you. Prayer is not a monologue; it's a dialogue. It's not just where you or God is doing all the talking but He wants to commune with you and have fellowship with you as well.

We need to maintain a spirit of faith and expectancy, for the kingdom of God functions by faith. By faith, we receive words from people who hear from God. By faith, we receive transmission that comes from heaven. To have hearing ears, we must believe that God is living inside us and speaking to us. We can hear His voice.

Hearing is so important for the Christian life. Hearing from God is so vitally important that our life totally depends on it.

John 10:27 says, "My sheep listen to my voice; I know them, and they follow me." I expect to hear His voice; I am His sheep. I don't think a lot of emphasis is put on Christian people hearing from God. I believe God wants to lead His children to some great things in life.

Let's look at this in the Amplified Bible. He said, "The sheep that are My own, hear and are listening to My voice, and I know them, and they follow Me." I don't know about you, but I think it's time we hear from God.

You need to learn to *tune* your hearing, like tuning a guitar. Balance and confirm what you hear with the teaching of scripture. The Word of God is going to tune your hearing. In other words, the more time you spend with the Word, the more it will help you tune into the spoken word. There is the *rhema* (spoken word), and there is the *logos* (written word). They are the same word in two different forms. Spend time with the *logos*, and it will tune your hearing to the *rhema*. When God speaks to you, you will know it's Him. And you will recognize Him because you've been spending time in the written word.

By saturating our minds in the Word of God, we tune our spiritual ears. When we start reading, meditating, and obeying the

Word of God, it prepares us to recognize God's voice. There's a true and unchanging *tone* of the Word of God. By spending time with the Word, we learn the true tone. We don't need to go around asking, "Is this me, or was that God? Was that me, or was that the devil?" When we get the tone from the Word, we will know it's God speaking to us. As we begin to develop perfect pitch in the Spirit, voices or messages containing any mixture of error or deception simply will not ring true when we develop perfect pitch.

This is how you get better hearing: wait for the peace of God. When you think you've heard something from God, wait for His peace. Let's look at Colossians 3:15 in the King James Version: "And let the peace that comes from Christ rule in your hearts." In the word *heart*, what are the first four letters? *Hear*. What are the first two letters? *He*. What are the last three letters? *Art*. So He put the ear in the center of your heart so you can hear Him, and that's the art of a Christian.

"And let the peace, the soul harmony which comes from Christ, rule, let it act as an umpire, peace acting like an umpire, deciding and settling with finality all questions that arise in your minds" (Colossians 3:15, AMP). What He says is that when you believe you've heard from God, let the umpire of peace call it safe or call it out. Follow your peace. Sometimes although the word you have heard in your spirit may line up perfectly with the Word of God, it may not be God's will for you, or it may not be time to act on that word. Therefore, learn to let the presence or the absence of the peace of God in your heart be the determining factor. Whatever you think you've heard, if there's no peace there, then the umpire is saying, "Hold up here. There's no peace there."

Peace is God's umpire that tells us whether a voice, a person, or a situation is safe. The absence of peace exposes lies and deception, but its presence confirms the voice or the will of God for our life. Therefore, do not act on the word you have heard unless your heart is filled with God's peace. You need to let the peace of God be your umpire.

Seek wise counsel.

Bold obedience.

God wants to talk to us. It is His will that we hear from Him. However, sometimes we may be so focused on our own problems that we can't hear what He's saying. There is never a problem with God speaking; the issue is always with something we may be doing to block His voice.

Barriers to hearing from Him include unbelief, having undeveloped spirits, and being burdened with an evil spirit that makes us spiritually deaf. Having a hardened conscience and neglecting to spend time with the Holy Spirit will also hinder our ability to hear from God. We keep our spiritual ears open by actively living in His Word so it can tune our spirits to Him. Allowing the Word to keep us clean from the world's influence enables us to detect the difference between truth and lies, thereby consistently defeating the enemy.

"Whatever we plant in our subconscious mind and nourish with repetition will one day become a reality" (Earl Nightingale).

"It's the repetition of affirmation that leads to belief. And once that belief becomes a deep conviction, things begin to happen" (Muhammad Ali).

"Repetition of the same thought or physical action develops into a habit which, repeated frequently enough, becomes an automatic reflex" (Norman Vincent Peale)

Rote learning is the process of memorizing information based on repetition. It enhances students' ability to quickly recall basic facts and helps develop foundational knowledge of a topic. Rote learning is the process of memorizing to be able to remember material verbatim.

Try to understand the information first. Information that is organized and makes sense to you is easier to memorize. If you find that you don't understand the material, spend some time understanding it before trying to memorize it.

Sleep on it. Studies show that your brain processes and stores information while you sleep. Try to review the information just before you go to sleep—even if it's only for a few minutes—and see if it helps embed the information into your memory.

14

They Said

Who told you that you were naked? the Lord God asked. Have you eaten from the tree whose fruit I commanded you not to eat? The man replied, it was the woman you gave me who gave me the fruit, and I ate it. Then the Lord God asked the woman, what have you done? The serpent deceived me, she replied, that's why I ate it.

—Genesis 3:11–13 (NLT)

There was a song I used to hear on the radio years ago called "I'm Still Holding On," written by Luther Barnes. One of the verses in the song stood out to me:

> *They said* I wouldn't make it,
> *They said* I wouldn't be here today,
> *They said* I'd never amount to anything.
> But I'm glad to say, that I'm on my way and I'm going more and more each day. There were many that started out with me but now they've gone astray, but I'm still holding on to His hand. (Emphasis mine)

I used to watch a lot of the Martin Lawrence show. There was an episode where he said, "If I tell you a duck could pull a truck, you gon' go and hook him up?" This was funny to me because most people, without really thinking about it, would believe it and probably would try it. LOL.

There was a popular saying called "they said." It was huge. It was always "they said" this, and "they said" that. They said, "Do this," and they said, "Do that." And if you followed pretty much what they said, you could probably end up in some difficult predicaments. You could end up believing and doing the wrong things, creating havoc for your life. I think you get the point.

I lived most of my life listening to what they said and found myself in some horrible situations. I lost opportunities, friendships, and many things that were pertinent to life. I found myself going after things that weren't good and were detrimental for me. What they said sometimes would give me a false sense of hope. We used to call them *pipe dreams*.

A lot of what they said was false propaganda—accusations of a person's sexual preference, gossips on how someone was making their money to pay their bills, and the spread of people's personal business. Most times, it was something negative and possibly incriminating. What they said has caused hurt feelings, wrong directions, and derailed futures.

Living by what they have said can leave us believing we are failures, unlovable, stupid, and worthless. A lot of this has been caused by whom we've been exposed to, our experiences over time, and what has been poured into us through our eye and ear gates.

This book expresses the importance of being careful about how, who, and what we are listening to. We must allow the Word of God to be the governing and primary source of information by which we live.

Clarence B. Skinner's Biography

Clarence is grounded in his spiritual life because of his God inspired Christian parents. His father was in a pastoral position and his mother was prayer worrier, they both were heavily active in the church they attended. His parents kept the family focused on God and living a Christ centered life. His siblings have embraced Clarence naturally and spiritually. They also have encouraged Clarence to share his anointed gift with others.

Throughout his life, Clarence has been known for his many talents. To name a few, Clarence is a creative writer, he writes songs and books. He sings, he's a musician and plays several instruments. He creates music, and he's a music producer. Over the years, Clarence's gifts have matured, blossomed, and surpassed expectations giving him more confidence to go further in his anointed gifts. Having been exposed to music at a very young age, Clarence has over 25 years of experience in the music arena as a musician, songwriter, and music producer.

Clarence's anointed gifts continue to develop and uplift others. He endeavors to pursue his love and passion for writing books, writing songs, and producing music. Clarence has taken on what he believes is his responsibility to aggressively minister through these anointed gifts.